Windows of the Heart

BARBARA BLAKE

Windows of the Heart

With a Foreword by
KITTY MUGGERIDGE

and illustrated by
Jan Nesbitt

Collins
FOUNT PAPERBACKS

Cover photograph by Maria Rees

First published in Great Britain
by Fount Paperbacks, London in 1986

Made and printed in Great Britain
by William Collins Sons & Co Ltd, Glasgow

Contents

Foreword

Whoever reads these meditations will find them an excellent guide to how to lead a Christian life in a pagan society. Some of them are short and some longer. In some God speaks directly to the reader, in others He speaks through the author.

They are simple and unpretentious and give us an impression of intimate confrontation with our Lord. They propose a way of finding happiness on earth by giving ourselves up to God and by doing what He wants us to do not what we want to, because He knows what is best for us.

Today's materialist society, madly in pursuit of happiness, urges us, by every means it can, to pursue our own devices and desires and to give ourselves up to self-fulfilment and self-interest. But if we pursue the modest proposal of these meditations, we shall find the only true happiness available in this life — which is to pursue God's will and not our own.

Kitty Muggeridge

1

The Peace Of God

Let not your heart be troubled. Rejoice! All is lent to you, it is not for you to possess. You are God's child.

Walk in His light.

Just as we cannot cry and truly pray at the same time, so it is impossible for us to go our own way in life and at the same time have the security and peace of God.

Real joy comes from peace of mind.

To have this peace we must surrender ourselves to God, give Him our wills, our problems – worries, resentments, sorrows, hopes, fears and so on. Then we must allow only positive thoughts into our minds.

Blessed are the pure in heart – those who keep the channel of their mind clear, for they shall see God. Indeed, they train themselves to see God everywhere.

Why do we choose tiredness, ill-health, worry, indecision, untidiness, the sense of never getting things done, loneliness and failure – all thoughts of self – when by the grace of God we can determine to go His way?

As thoughts beget actions, let us make sure that these are God-guided.

We can spread happiness by being happy; but real joy only comes when we have a clear conscience.

Let us learn to have times when we keep the mind still – not a stagnant quiet, but one of dynamic radiance. Visualize that "light which lighteth every man that cometh into the world".

There can only be peace of mind where God is our total security.

You cannot only deal with a situation while you are worrying about it. When you have faithfully surrendered it to God you will be shown His way for you in His time.

We can only see our reflection clearly in a pool when the water is still.

So, only when our minds are still, at peace, can we ourselves be used to reflect God.

A busy day, yet we should still be serene.

If we are really listening to the divine voice we shall be directed at all times, even in the smallest things. Our lives will flow; the Holy Spirit will work in us as we try sincerely to follow the path.

We have the love of God, His joy and peace, when we live in the awareness of His presence.

Nothing can affect the man who is spiritually poised, for he owns but one master.

Make haste slowly. This may sound paradoxical, but surely means that when we are poised in awareness of the presence of God, trying only to do His will, we shall not be nervy and hurried, our self-will leading us here and there. Instead, through the grace of God, we shall live an ordered life.

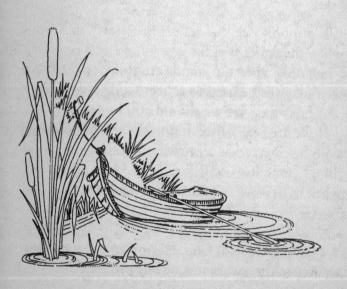

The way of God is not one of strain. Living consciously for Him and with Him creates balance and harmony which others can feel, and this peace, which is an expanding quality, can spread indefinitely.

Heaven and earth are full of the glory of God, though we so often blind our eyes to this. We are apt to dwell on misery, ill-health and physical death, and we often lose the spiritual path.

Let us throw off the worries that chain us, accept God, and in humility learn to live as He intends, in utter dependence on Him.

Before, we were slaves to our moods and outside influences; now, we shall be stabilized by our peace of mind.

"Fear not, for I am with you" (Isaiah 43:5). This is not idle saying but the living – past, present and future – truth.

"If God be for us, who can be against us?" (Romans 8:13).

Then let us surrender our human will, accept Him and put Him first in our lives.

Blessed is he who keeps his inner gaze on God and who does not live merely by the senses.

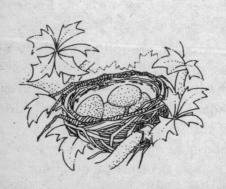

What audacity we have in allowing our human wills to rule our lives! We plan, we arrange, then — however much we achieve on the human level — we feel dissatisfaction and wonder why.

Man is divided into three parts — spiritual, mental, physical. If we do not develop the spiritual, we shall be unbalanced, unhappy.

When we are divinely attuned we shall be at peace.

It is now that counts, the eternal now, so let us keep the mind clear, allowing no anxiety or other negative thought to enter.

When we are fully loving God we cannot be resentful or jealous, neither can we be afraid, for "perfect love casteth out fear".

How easy to slip from the path – a little unkind gossip, a dismal thought, envy, self-pity . . . the list is long, and in a flash we can lose the awareness of the presence of God.

Let us concentrate on God and His will, not on *our* thoughts, *our* shortcomings. So may our greatest desire be to love and serve Him every moment.

With what strain do we often achieve our

object! Where is the joyful smooth-running life when our days are full of flurry and unrest? Where is the peace of God we can reflect to others?

Only in continual dependence of God can we be used by Him.

We are within infinity now. In spite of appearances, all around us is the hushed atmosphere, the all-love of infinite God.

Man alone has made chaos on this earth by his thoughts.

Breathe deeply of this all-pervading love and peace of God, His strength and righteousness.

Let us go forth buoyed up by the knowledge that "underneath are the everlasting arms" (Deuteronomy 33:27).

Everlasting life is ours whether we like to believe it or not, so surely it is for each of us to live in the way destined for us. Why do we keep on making the same mistakes, get into such difficulties, when all the time the only answer to life is always waiting for each one of us?

While we live in our own human strength we continue to suffer, to feel desperate and alone.

When we accept God in our lives and try to follow Him in all things, there is an immediate change. Our peace of mind is the greatest joy on earth, that "peace which passeth understanding" (Philippians 4:7). It is like a fountain of living water. But we are to keep the channel of our minds clear. All negative thinking must go before that living water can sustain us.

The phrase "I am a jealous God" is much misunderstood. God made us and wants us to live as He ordained. He is "jealous" for our good — and besides, he wants a perfect world.

Let us go our way in peace, rejoicing in the knowledge that God is with us now and always.

2

Surrender To God

It is only when we give up the struggle, knowing ourselves utterly beaten, and then surrender our lives to God, that we start to live. We must lose our lives to find them.

Do we stop to consider the love of God? It is there for us, as is His strength.

Alas, how we strive on our own; what a sense of loneliness we endure as we battle on instead of allowing God to take over for us. So may we remember these words: Let go and let God.

Let us be empty of self and full of the love of God.

It is *how we* do something which counts in the spiritual life, not *what* we do. This means that our attitude of mind is all-important.

Are we continually loving God, therefore relaxed, or are we in a state of "I must get this job done"? If we are in this last state, pause. Just think, are we ready should someone in trouble call? Of course not: we ourselves would be spiritually dry. Maybe we should smother the caller with self-willed sympathy based only on emotion.

Let us seek the Lord and His will every moment. The joy and adventure in so doing is unbelievable.

We all need true humility. If we really love God, if we listen for His will and obey, we shall be humble-minded, and self will be forgotten.

Bitterness is a sign of spiritual immaturity, and the man who is bitter is his own enemy. He may not know what harm he is doing to himself and others, for bitterness is contagious. No wonder he is often lonely.

But if he accepts God in his life, there will be no more bitterness.

When we completely rely on God, our sense of "It all depends on me" changes to – "Lord, I depend on You".

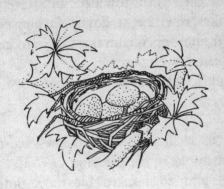

It was ordained for man to have lightness of heart, and this can only be achieved when the conscience is clear.

"But look at my life," you may say, "all that has happened; how I suffer and what So-and-So has done to me . . ."

Yes, but if we hang on to resentment, depression or the thought of ill-health, we have no lightness of heart. How can we have?

Think of the early Christians, and many later ones known for their lightness of heart in the face of martyrdom!

If we want the indwelling life of God to be made

manifest in us we must let this divine power flow freely. Our own petty thinking will have to go, likes, dislikes, resentment, gossip, lovelessness for others and even for ourselves. We are to go with the tide of life, not against it.

It is God first, let us remember.

We need to clear our consciousness countless times to be aware of the presence of God, to hear His voice and to receive blessings both for ourselves and for others through us.

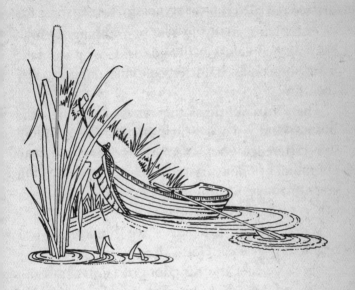

We are like someone who climbs to the ship's bridge and takes the wheel. How dare we try to navigate the vessel! Is it any wonder that the ship founders on the rocks?

And all the time the Captain is there ready to take command – waiting.

Stop Thief! "Oh, pickpockets, bank robbers and so on are thieves", we may say smugly. But wait — are we not also thieves?

There are many ways of robbing besides stealing people's worldly goods. Gossip can take away someone's character, continual unpunctuality their time.

There are countless other ways of stealing — the unsaid kindly word which would have made all the difference to someone in depression, the compliment not passed on. If we live in resentment or a turmoil of hurry, this can affect others and take away their peace.

Worst of all, whenever we think and live negatively we steal God's time.

"Seek ye first the Kingdom of God", says the Lord, and if we do so we shall use His days as He wills, not as we choose.

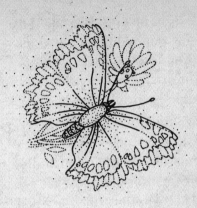

It is *being* which counts in the spiritual life, not the constant *doing*. By right being, right doing follows automatically.

If we are truly humble we shall not attempt to do one thing ourselves without first being aware of the presence of God.

"Ho, everyone that thirsteth, come ye to the waters" (Isaiah 55:1) – the waters of peace, love, strength and guidance. Only these waters will quench the thirst we have had since birth.

In accepting Him, surrendering ourselves

entirely to His will and keeping His presence uppermost in our minds, we shall find our permanent thirst quenched.

Each of us, unique in personality, is but a fragment of this divinely-made creation. Let us stop all wandering thoughts, including those of non-achievement, non-progress. We are asked not to judge. This applies to our judgement of ourselves too. We are His, and He is actually within us. Let us try to express Him, allowing nothing unlike Him – and that includes worry – to remain in the consciousness.

As, wonder upon wonders, we are made in the image and likeness of God, we are required to give Him everything of ourselves – our entire life.

We may go through life without realizing the nearness of God. How hard to miss such joy and peace, how aimless life can seem, how worthless the struggle; and for those who wish to tread the spiritual path, it is doubly hard.

Let us, like Peter walking on the waves, take a step in faith; make the spiritual experiment of accepting and loving God, depending only on Him. Let us try for five minutes, for an hour, for a week . . .

Let us keep turning to God, surrendering ourselves, everyone and everything to Him. Thus anxiety is avoided with all strain and self-interest. By the grace of God, blessings can then flow to us and through us for others.

Sometimes we may allow ourselves to be influenced negatively by people, or we may sink into depression, resentment, self-pity – all these and other killers of which we may be quite unconscious.

Let us throw out such dangerous thoughts. They drain us of the spiritual power destined for each of us. Let us turn to God and re-surrender our lives to Him – and that includes our thinking.

Behold the love of God, yet our self-will persists. We let the eye direct us instead of listening to the will of God. Stop doing what *you* think are good actions, and see what He wants of you, and when. Therein lies your health and happiness, not in spasmodic efforts, however kindly meant.

Petition, petition. Is that the way to live for God — only asking, begging?

Considering all our blessings, it's a pretty poor way.

How often do we say "thank you", and why can't we say it often? Always, it seems, our own human wills take over. When shall we surrender our wills to God in every facet of our lives? Only then can there be no strain or fear.

Let us this day make an act of faith, an experiment if you like — from now on to do everything for God and with God. Let us spend time in realizing that His love for us is infinite. Let us spend time in loving Him and receiving His love as healing power permeating our being.

Then we can say, "Nothing of me: I am a channel for the love of God."

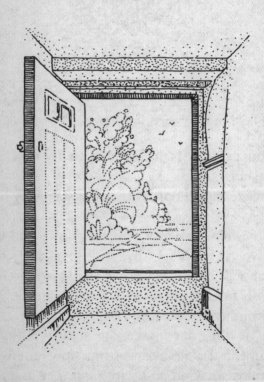

Childish or childlike? What a difference — one full
of self-will, the other full of trust.

Which are we?

3

Learning and Serving

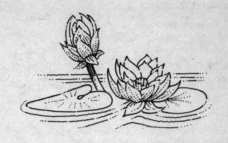

Every moment lived consciously in the awareness of the presence of God is one of fresh spiritual opportunity and adventure. In the past there were so many things we dared not do. Now, when only trying to follow the divine will, we are ready to face anything . . . with Him.

It is only when I know I am utterly nothing that God can use me fully.

If we insist on leaving God and His goodness out of our lives, we shall find that life defeats us.

49

We shall indeed be lonely, continue to suffer and do battle, until we first accept God, and then go with life, not against it.

While we go our way, think our thoughts, do we realize that we are keeping God waiting?

If we keep on taking back what we have given to God, we shall have confusion in our lives.

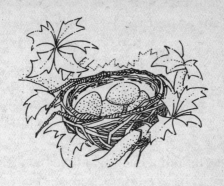

Today is a fragment of life eternal. May it be as God wills, not as we will.

Stop! Not all the obvious things waiting to be done may be His wish for us at this moment. Let us be alert, ready. Somebody in need may cross our path. If we are entirely engrossed in our own efforts, we may miss opportunities for God.

Awake O soul! By His grace we have the incredible privilege of working for and with Him. This is no presumption for we "are the branches". "I am the vine", our Lord says (John 15:1).

Let us remember that we can do nothing without the vine.

If only we would take what is offered by God, what happiness and well-being could be ours, and what blessings would flow through us to others.

To protect ourselves from wind and weather we wear overcoats.

In life, are we strong enough to withstand the evil forces around us? How dare we live without a spiritual overcoat? Only if so cloaked with the armour of God are we safe and ready to be used for His purpose.

Let us show forth the love and joy of God in this life, which has been lent to us for His service.

Let us speak nothing without our mind turned God-ward, do nothing, think nothing. In this way we shall live in and with Him.

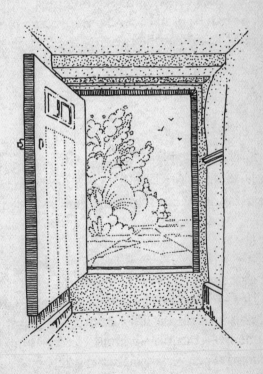

Thanks be to God for every chance to serve Him, whether from an invalid bed or by going forth into the world.

"I am not doing anything, not being used to help anyone", a patient in hospital might say. But by his very being, his thinking and praying, he can be used. As events and personalities cross his mind, he can be used to send out love and blessing to them — to reflect the love of God.

Each day gives us a new chance to express the glory of God and His goodness. Let us waste no more opportunities for Him. We are His instruments — He has no hands or feet but ours. What a privilege we have — what a responsibility!

Yet do we express God . . . or self?

Let us remember it is how we go through a situation that counts in the spiritual life, not what happens, so our thoughts are all-important. May we keep them turned God-ward.

If we deny God we deny ourselves and others, for if we fail to keep turning to Him, we are responsible for much suffering. While we think our thoughts opportunities pass us by, blessings which we reject for ourselves *and* through us for others.

Conscience tells us what we should do. Self-will tells us what we want to do.

OUR FAULTS AND FAILINGS

Shyness: Some people go through life a prisoner to shyness. What hell this is! Entering crowded rooms alone, sitting opposite passengers in buses or trains, they act a part to hide the agony of shyness, and so, missing out on life, they suffer increasingly. They are frequently misunderstood.

But shyness is a concentration on self, however much the victim hates this. It is a looking in instead of out.

Let us remember that we are like stones in God's mosaic, each one equal and necessary to form this perfect pattern. We are *all* precious in His sight.

Loneliness: Unless we have experienced true loneliness, we cannot know its meaning, its desolation and continuity.

We can be lonely with no one present. We can be lonely in a crowd of friends.

But instead of looking inwards let us try to do something about it, for loneliness can be a spiritual advantage.

We can never be truly alone when we are with God. No longer need we rely on people or circumstances. Our petty prides, ambitions, hurts and resentments are swallowed up in an overwhelming, outpouring love for God which embraces the world. Our desire is to listen for His will, not our own, and to obey Him instantly.

What freedom from life's shackles for those who achieve this, even spasmodically – what indescribable joy! Even in solitary confinement, we can be used to give out love and blessing. Then there will be no time for loneliness.

Possessiveness: Trying to possess is immature. It is a phase in our development.

As we advance spiritually we learn to "give over" our friendships, ideas, possessions. We no longer break our hearts over a smashed ornament, as we once did over a favourite toy.

We go with life, not against it.

Indignation: To live the spiritual life there is no time for indignation. While we hold forth about someone whom we consider has let us down, or persecuted us, we may put off those who believe we have something of great value, an inner peace and guidance. We could be used instead to send out love, and to bring great blessing upon the whole situation. There may be something in ourselves which has reacted on the other person, our own spiritual lack and failure to reflect the love of God. There may be a divine reason for what has happened, lessons to be learned. We may have been relying too much on a fellow being, instead of on God.

Let us pray for those who "despitefully use us" (Luke 6:28), not condemn them. This is our opportunity to reflect the love of God.

Jealousy: This can cause agonies of suffering as we try to hold on to what we believe is ours.

It is only when we surrender everything, including friendship, to God, that we obtain peace of mind.

Look around at those who are jealous, possessive; their fears and behaviour often induce the loved one to escape from them.

"Seek ye first the kingdom of God and His righteousness" (Luke 12:31), what He wants us to be, to think, to do. Then there will be no more jealousy.

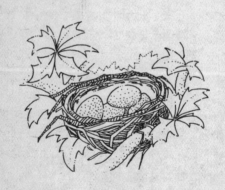

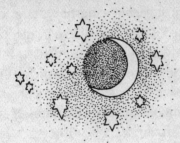

Boastfulness: We should pity the man who boasts, not condemn him. He is very insecure. Wanting love and encouragement, he tries to impress others, and people with perception just leave him. He can be very lonely.

Are we in some way to blame? In an atmosphere of criticism, with little or no love, he may feel so "starved" that to build up his ego he starts name-dropping, and talking big.

If he had been in God-consciousness he would not have wanted to do this; and had we also been, we should not have created the atmosphere which caused him to show off.

Doubt: We know the story of Peter walking on the water and our Lord reproving him for his lack of faith when he fell. Let us also look up and keep our gaze on God, not on the raging waters, which in our case can be confusion, distrust, dismay.

We should always put the Lord first. Instead of trying so hard to succeed in the world, let us strive to love and serve Him every moment. Then we shall be fulfilling our destiny, drawing blessing on ourselves and, through us, to others.

Hurt Feelings: If we are hurt beyond words, let us not sink into depression, resentment, self-pity, but claim our heritage as sons or daughters of God.

Let us pray for those who wrong us, and see them too as God's children.

Then we shall be lifted from the abyss of self-obsession.

Being Free: A balloonist casts out ballast to rise higher, and if we would progress in the spiritual life, we too must cast off the shackles which bind us. Many of these are in the memory.

"Oh, if only that hadn't happened . . . ", we

say. Yet it is not for us to feel guilty or condemned all our lives. Let us remember that our Lord Jesus Christ, by His grace, His sacrifice, has taken away the sins of the world – including ours.

Let us have a truly contrite heart; in humility accept God and ask His forgiveness, then realize we are immediately forgiven. Then, for His sake, let us forgive ourselves and all others, and, where possible, make amends.

Criticism: We are told "judge not", yet also "be wise as serpents". Sometimes it is right to criticize constructively. Let us see this is done in love – the love of God. We should never try to appear on a higher level than the one we criticize.

How often has constructive, loving criticism been the turning point for good in a man's life!

We can be so blind to our own faults and failings, and if someone points them out, how humbly grateful we should be.

There are few who invite criticism, and alas, few who receive it with thanks.

"Blessed are the meek" (Matthew 5:5) – those who have learned to control temper and moods, who do not take offence, but are preoccupied instead in keeping the awareness of the presence of God.

Let us rise out of material thinking and greet each new experience with joy. When we cease our planning, our arranging, and depend solely on God we shall see how He undertakes for us.

Spread the Good News: Besides the Church, and those called entirely to evangelism, are not we, whoever we are (and whatever we have or have not done), also to spread the Good News? Are not we also to be used to save souls?

How shall we feel in the after-life when we realize our unfulfilled responsibilities towards other people?

"But I'm hopeless," we may say, "no example. I'm ill, old, inadequate. What do I know about . . . ?"

But if we have received much, then much is expected of us. We cannot "blow hot and cold", cannot try to lead a Christian life and yet do nothing about other people.

It may be that we only need to pray for them.

When we love and serve God wholeheartedly, He will direct us in all things.

Love is the fulfilling of the law. Keep the awareness of the presence of God at all times, then you will be guided how to live in that love.

Realize your spiritual identity. How we forget, and think and act in our human way, when, all the time, by the grace of God, we have access to the divine mind and guidance.

God never gives us a task too difficult. When it is His will all things are possible, so go forward in that knowledge and truth. Rejoice with thanksgiving.

Turn away thoughts of loneliness and self-pity.
Claim your spiritual identity as a son, a
daughter of God.
Rely on no one and nothing but Him,
for "He careth for you" (Peter 5:7).

O glorious destiny unfolding! Only in total obedience to the inner prompting of the Most High can we attain to that for which we were born. Lift up your heart and know. Keep your gaze on the mountain peak, not in the valleys. Then shall darkness flee away as morning follows night; then shall your soul be glad and rejoice.

Let us try to live constantly in the awareness of the presence of God for His is the kingdom, the power and the glory.

4

God's Way

The way of God or our way – the choice is always with us, the time to choose, Now.

Man has a thirst for spiritual enlightenment, whether he knows it or not.

Let us no longer be slaves to ourselves, but turn to God and claim our birthright as His sons, His daughters.

There are many who never think of the hereafter or ask for what purpose they are here – which is to make manifest the Kingdom of God on earth.

Let us rejoice that we have the right and privilege of going the way God has ordained for us.

Two roads always lie ahead of us — *our* way or the way God ordained for us. We have the choice.

We know what happens if we choose *our* way — the often empty success, regrets, longings, depression, the feeling of a wasted life. No wonder we make so many mistakes and suffer so much!

Or in childlike faith we can choose to do the will of God and stay in the awareness of His near presence, with its love, peace, joy, strength, purpose and adventure.

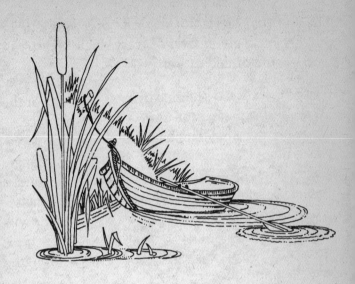

It is all or nothing with the Kingdom of God, and there can be no off-times for us at all.

Here and now let us decide to live for Him in every moment.

Today let us not waste God's time, because this is what we do during our lone struggles. May we rather keep on loving Him and dwelling in the knowledge that He is everywhere. By diligent practice this can become our way of thinking, our way of life.

The spiritual life is not just one of saying daily prayers, but a giving over of every single breath to God – a life of dedication.

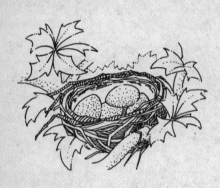

What a difference there is at once in health and spirits when one lives for the Lord instead of for self, however many "good deeds" we may have tried on our own.

O, the joy of depending on One who cannot let us down! We are able to achieve things which formerly we could not or dared not do. Now we are actually led by Him!

Everlasting life is ours, so surely it is time we led our lives in the way we know we should. No more day-dreaming — all the might-have-beens and regrets. That train of thought is destructive, negative.

God is all. Let us give everything over to Him, surrender our thoughts and, from henceforth, reflect His love, peace and strength.

We are upheld in the eternal changelessness, for whatever we may think or do, God does not change.

5

Words of
Encouragement

To be at peace with yourself and all men you must first be at peace with Me.

It is not too late. It is never too late for man to turn in complete humility and sincerity to Me.

Every moment you have the opportunity to start again to love Me and to follow My will for you.

Did you think I could desert you? It is you who have deserted Me, by putting people and things first.

Do not try to run by yourself, for therein lies danger and disillusionment. Seek me.

Do not make an idol of anyone or anything. Have no gods but Me.

The choice is always yours — self-will or My will. If you choose your will you become a prisoner to self.

Only when you let go of your last human security can I use you fully.

When you remember that you are My child, actually part of Me, you cannot feel alone.

A pool of water can only reflect if clear and calm. So, too, only if your mind is clear of self can it reflect My love.

87

Peace of mind can only come through complete dependence on Me, complete love and obedience. Then you cannot be afraid, for perfect love casts out fear, My light will shine through you, and others will feel its warmth. But only in giving out this radiance of joy and peace can you retain it.

Are you prepared to be utterly humble this day, ready to carry out any menial task for Me? Are you ready to give up anything you may be doing should I wish – prepared to be completely obedient to My will? Without this, O child of many distractions, I cannot use you fully.

Love Me, desire Me, talk to Me inwardly; and thus keeping the mind occupied with positive attitudes, you will admit no harmful thoughts.

When you can love those you find it most difficult to love, you are loving Me most.

If you want Me in your life you must give up all to My service and, in love and humility, follow Me.

Seek nothing more than to love and please Me.
How can you be ready to do My will if you are
always planning what *you* want to do, however
good the intention? You will be unable to hear My
voice, My will for you.

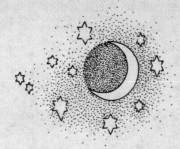

Although you are told "bear ye one another's burdens" (Galatians 6:2), first realize My presence. How else can you hope to be used to help another except through Me? With Me all things are possible. So can you use My strength, not your self-will.

In worry and haste you cannot hear My voice. All will be well if after accepting Me you love, listen and obey Me.

When serving Me to your utmost you have no one and nothing to fear, for you have only one Master. But remember, service for Me is a whole-time occupation, a lifetime's dedication.

Reach up – leave your anxieties with Me. Do you think you can arrange your life? It is loaned to you as is everything else.

You and all men are stewards of what you think you possess; yet you are My sons and daughters. Do not try to steal from Me, for that is what you do when you go *your* way and use life for *your* purpose.

All is Mine. All is ever Mine. Listen for My voice and I will tell you what to do.

See Me only. Hear Me only. Abide in Me as I, remember, abide in you. There can then be no sense of alone-ness, no loneliness, for you will do everything for Me and with Me.

That way you will have strength, My strength.

Love me actively, not a spasmodic and emotional outpouring, but a steady loving. Then there will be balance in your life. Man was made for love. In loving Me you love all creation. No more are you as a storm-tossed vessel on the tide of life. You are My son, My daughter.

When you live by prayer, which is conscious union with Me, you will know My will, even in the smallest things.

You are used to thinking by human standards. With me all things are possible.

Before you think and act, remember I am here. So be aware of My presence, as I, remember, am always conscious of you.

Pray for all men; forgive all men. How dare you not, for I forgive you.

I am the God of love, and with Me there is no room for anything but love.